The Pre-Marital Counselor's Handbook

Lascelle W Robinson

THE PUBLISHER'S
NOTEBOOK LIMITED
"ENVISION IT, WE'LL PUBLISH IT"

2018

THE PRE-MARITAL COUNSELOR'S HANDBOOK

Copyright © 2017. Lascelle W Robinson

For information contact :

Lascelle W Robinson

PO Box 7, Montego Bay #1, PO

St James, Jamaica WI

Email: facefacts02@yahoo.com

Cover Design: Lascelle Robinson

ISBN : 978-976-96192-3-4

ISBN: 978-976-96062-1-0 (first publication)

Publisher: The Publisher's Notebook Limited

Email: **publisher@thepublishersnotebook.com**

Website: **http://thepublishersnotebook.com**

THE PUBLISHER'S
NOTEBOOK LIMITED
" ENVISION IT, WRI I PUBLISH IT"

Dedicated to:

Kardia, Karyn & Zahir

CONTENTS

Foreword

Over many conversations with Lascelle, I began to understand why it was so important he got it right. He understood that marriage is sacred and is the cornerstone of the greatest institution that exists. Even more importantly, he understood that for marriage to withstand the test of time, couples must get it right from the very beginning.

This body of work is about making sure the right people end up together for the right reasons, so they may stay together despite all the reasons that could tear them apart.

The in-depth approach to finding ways to provoke and challenge couples to examine themselves before attaching themselves to each other is the conscious effort of this book to awaken couples to the reality of *till death do us part*.

This book will make you pause and become mindful and intentional about every decision you make about the most important partnership into which you will venture.

Jacqueline Bernard, MA, LPC - Clinical Psychotherapist,
Adjunct Professor of Psychology, Northhampton Community College

Preface

In the beginning, God created Adam from the dust of the earth and Eve from Adam. The next human being on earth was 'created' by mankind. Certainly, the ability to procreate has given mankind almost god-like status.

This power has been used to hurt, maim, cripple, embarrass, create divisions, destroy families, topple governments, brought kings to their knees, make children hopeless, weakened the fittest and turn the wise into fools.

Intimate relationships come with responsibilities and for this reason, one has to be prepared to assume its demands. An individual or couple should never think that there is a God-sent right person made for them and for this reason God will preserve their relationship. Remember that Adam and Eve were individually perfect, and they destroyed their relationship and the world. They had no choice, but we do.

If you do not know how to handle dynamite do not light the fuse!

Acknowledgments

With gratitude, I salute all those who have helped to make this book a reality.

I especially thank my family, friends and those who allowed me to include their experiences in this project.

Introduction

Jesus said, "The Spirit of the Lord *is* upon me, because he hath anointed [and] sent me to heal the brokenhearted, (Luke 4:18 KJV emphasis added)

Hearts, like bones, can also be broken and as the bone requires medical procedures the heart also needs a specialist. It would appear from the above example of Jesus that Christians with the skill set are being called to attend to hopeless and broken hearts.

The Pre-Marital Counselor's Handbook is designed to aid those who are interested in providing counsel to individuals and couples who are considering intimate relationship and marriage respectively.

The theological interpretation of marriage, divorce, and remarriage is developed from the Christian's Old and New Testament narratives. While all may not be used, investigative questions have also been employed to stimulate relevant discussion in the counsel sessions.

Rookie

One year after I was assigned to my first pastorate, I assisted a couple in getting married. Three days later I was asked to intervene in their domestic dispute.

As I sat in their home, I asked my first question, "How long were you together before you got married?" "Fourteen years, Sir," the bride replied. "And how long have you been fighting?" I continued. "Fourteen years Sir," she said. They were divorced a year after and I did not do any more weddings for the next four years.

I was devastated.

During those silent years, my heart wandered in its own wilderness and my inexperienced plagued me. I called a colleague and explained how badly I felt. He assured me that I should not make much of it, as I was not responsible for their problems.

I believed him but still could not understand how my heart should not be concerned. I encouraged and participated in their union. For years I searched for answers through research, observation of the type and content of premarital counseling; informally interviewing pastors and prospective brides and grooms.

I came to one conclusion, if I had asked the appropriate questions before I instructed them to say, "I Do," and had gotten the same answers, I would have given a different recommendation.

Not only did my inexperience injure their lives but also their children's and their in-laws. When I agreed to put them together, I shared in their choice and lifelong decision.

Since then I have learned that many are taken before the altar to be joined in Holy Matrimony without substantial and professional counseling. The paradox is that these couples are told that they should not enter marriage inadvisably, by the same official who never offered them, counsel.

Like a car dealer who sells motorcars and does not have service personnel, stocked parts, and accessories, the church strongly encourages and at times forces people into marriages, usually to prevent fornication. Marriage in itself does not prevent fornication, for this is an individual responsibility.

The principle and structure behind marriages, especially in the Old Testament, was to preserve cultures, increase tribal population, produce breadwinners and warriors to protect tribes. It appears as if the collective consciousness of some churches is to use marriage to prevent fornication, instead of teaching and promoting the importance of self-control, respecting one's body as God's temple, and the importance of singularity before marriage. After an individual has accepted Jesus as Lord and Saviour, the next step in God's salvation plan is not marriage, that choice rests with the couple and not the Church.

While some churches seek fame for healing diseases and broken bones, Jesus begs for the healing of emotional and spiritual broken hearts. "The Spirit of the Lord is upon me because he hath anointed me to...heal the brokenhearted..." (Luke 4:18). To provide emotional health care, the church must have a purposeful after-marriage-care-program which is staffed by God-gifted and trained personnel.

In his instructions to Titus (2:2-5) Paul told him to encourage the experienced women to teach the younger women to be good wives. From Paul's instruction, it seems as if he wanted Titus to build a community program where young girls were to be taught how to be good wives. While the Proverbs are probabilities, not promises, the writer declared, "Whoso findeth a wife findeth a good thing, and obtaineth favour of the LORD" (Proverbs 18:22).

Then continuing his instruction, in Titus 3:2, he said that a bishop must be the husband of one wife and be able to teach. From a contextual perspective, it seems as if Paul is also emphasizing the point that men, especially those in Church authority, must be exemplary in marriage and be able to teach the subject.

It is, therefore, my hope that the information in this book will:

- assist the couple in examining their choice to be married; who is chosen and possibly reconsider their final decision.

- help the couple to examine their level of maturity and each other's readiness to face the unpredictable consequences of a shared life.

- help the couple understand and accept the meaning of Christian Marriage and the capacity to carry out consent.

Like medicine interacting with ones' body chemistry relationships have emotional, social and psychological side effects, *so face the facts and forget fictions,* "I Do" carries permanent lifelong implications.

True Stories

Dudley & Atoya

The following is a testimony from one of the first couples I counseled after I resumed my counseling sessions. I asked them to tell of their pre-marital counseling experience.

"We knew each other for two years before we started dating. We are both pastors' children and were quite mindful of the responsibility and the reputation we bore. We dated for five years, then informed our fathers of our mutual emotional interest.

We officially got engaged six months prior to the date we planned to get married. We were strongly advised to get counsel and Lascelle Robinson was highly recommended. Looking back, we should have done the counseling, prior to our public announcement.

Our first session was rather intrusive. The questions went right to the core of our relationship.

For some questions, we either didn't know how to answer or didn't want to answer, especially in the presence of each other. For example, we were asked, "What is it about the other person that you don't like or what annoyed you?" Really! Who would want to answer such a question after setting a marriage date?

Well, from that first session, we realized that there were things we either thought about but were afraid to say to each other or we just didn't want to face our realities. However, it was in that first session we realized how important it was for us to know and voice these things before we committed ourselves. The interview session really got us thinking.

By the end of the first session, we felt unsure as to our former decision to get married. We started questioning if this was right for us. That weekend, we hardly spoke to each other which was quite unusual as we would normally spend hours and hours chatting and laughing. In fact, Atoya said she spent the time in deep self-searching while tears washed away the weekend.

Other questions that got us thinking more seriously about our proposed marriage included checking our family's background (if there was any relationship, money management, health issues, physical, etc.)

For us, even the aspect of how we individually spent was not a concern, our focus was really to get married. Now it appeared that a lot of things will have to be done differently. No longer what "I" want or was accustomed to, but, *we* and *us*, managing a single home.

Bombarded by these perspectives and information, in such a short time, before the wedding, made us really stop and think whether we were indeed ready for marriage.

As we continued the sessions, our faith was lifted, and we realized it was not all gloom. We were now discovering that what we shared, as a couple, went beyond mere attraction and that gave us hope that we could actually make it.

We knew we had to get counsel but not at this intense level. In retrospect, we are so happy that we did. Since the first interview and subsequent sessions, we found out things about each other that we did not know for the seven years we were together. Maybe we took a lot of things for granted, about each other, because we are Christians. In one of the sessions, we learnt that perfect Adam and perfect Eve destroyed a perfect world.

We also understood some possible reasons why some persons, especially young couples struggled so much. We became more determined that we would not be among the ones that fell by the wayside. We realized that we had to have reasonable expectations and not live in the fairytale that we see on TV or read in novels.

During the sessions, Atoya's mind went beyond the wedding day and night to actually live together, taking care of a home, a husband and maybe even children! Plus working full time. Was she ready for this? Could she deal with my snoring, picking up after me; would I be able to handle her mood swings? We did a lot of thinking and thinking and some more thinking.

Would we recommend counseling to others? After this counseling experience, the answer is a RESOUNDING YES. We would definitely recommend to anyone who plans to get married really get counseling.

An attempt to measure the relevance of counseling and how it informed us cannot be quantified, as it did more for us than we could ever have dreamed. However, for the purposes of this exercise, we would say 11 out of 10.

Before the sessions, we expected to be asked if we loved each other or if it was infatuation and stuff along that line. We were jolted and at the same time pleasantly surprised at the scope of the questions. Each question dug deeper and deeper into the core of our relationship, an unwelcome step by step invasion.

Well, we came through thankful for the thorough questioning that caused us to discover our own answers. On August 18, 2013, we celebrated 6 years of marriage and it has been GREAT! Sure, we've had challenges, but we were able to appropriately handle them. There were times when it seemed we lost sight of each other, but with our determination to make our marriage work and to enjoy the journey, we found our way back again.

We must add, being Christians have helped us to weather a lot of storms that could have toppled our relationship. It is also important that both persons share the same religious belief.

The fact that both of us do not believe in divorce and remarriage has motivated us to work through our issues rather than trying to find another way out. Also, having the Lord Jesus Christ as the first person in our relationship has also helped, as a threefold cord is not easily broken.

Jesus has become our Hope and our Rock. Having a relationship with Him, as individuals, before we got married has helped. It does not mean that persons who are unsaved cannot have good relations too, but God adds another dimension to our lives. Knowing that our lives together pleased Him and knowing that He is there to help in times of need is a wonderful assurance and added bonus."

Dudley & Atoya

Silently Suffering

The following is a true account from a young wife who is experiencing extreme difficulty in her marriage. As you read, please note her reasons for getting married, her thought processes and their results. Do not be condemning but as you read, you may judge her actions based on the Word, but also keep her in your prayers. Ask yourself, is it possible for this to happen to me? How can I avoid going through this experience? If I were in her situation, what would I do? Also, consider the husband's situation and ask yourself, if you were, he, do you think you would be aware or want to be aware of what is going on?

"I have been a Christian since I was 17 years old. I got married at age 20 because it was the thing to do, as a Christian, and to prevent fornication.

Three years before my marriage I had broken off a relationship with another guy out of town and started to look around for someone else. Of course, many persons at church said I was a good marriage material.

I decided to settle with the best one and we immediately began planning our wedding. Our first and last counseling session was on the day of our wedding, during the marriage ceremony.

I got married and moved in with a man for the first time in my life. Sex that night was a must because that was what was supposed to happen - I got pregnant that same night.

After eighteen years of sleepless months, torturing weeks and nerve-racking days, I am still wondering what I have gotten myself into. I got married because it was the Christian thing to do; I chose the best guy and I know he is still a good person. But now I realize that I did not love him, still, don't, never will and I cannot hurt him with the truth!

My suffering became more severe about six years after my wedding. This was when, for the first time, I really got the chance to move around and meet different guys and even explored what different relationships would be like. As a result of my emotional expedition, I did find the love of my life.

We have been together for ten years now and the joy he represents is the only thing that is keeping my actual marriage. Sexual intercourse could not be better, and I have buried every ounce of guilt because this has been what I have always wanted. I know that I am doing wrong but how else can I be happy?

The limit on our relationship has become increasingly painful because we cannot see each other all the time and when we do, in public, we cannot even hold each other the way we want. Day and night, we talk by text or voice and he preserves my joy for each morning.

My husband knows that I am withdrawn and by now he suspects that I do not love him. I have not said anything to him, but any fool would know, and he is not one. From time to time, though, he would let me know that he understands that I am under a lot of pressure, from work! The only pressure I am under is my commitment to this marriage vow.

We were both taught that divorce is a sin and we believe it. I am in this marital prison because I said I do to the one I should not have said it to. Now I am living a regrettable lie because I absolutely do not have feelings for him. I really wish someone had said to me that I did not have to marry at the time I did.

I know that my husband has great potential, but I want to be with someone I am in love with. My husband has the ability to reach the stars, but he needs help to get there and I cannot help him; I have no desire for him nor his dreams. As a matter of fact, the less he talks to me the better I feel.

My lover is single, and I am so afraid that one day he may get frustrated and move on with someone and leave me here in this emotional hell. If my husband would just die, I know I would be able to live. But he won't die! I know God would not answer that prayer, so I have not prayed it anymore, but from time to time I know God hears my wish.

My life itself is at a standstill. The emotional weight of my husband in my life prevents me from being me, in full flight. Oh, how I wish I was really truly me. Every day I have to pretend as if I love him especially when we are in public. When, oh Lord, will I get to be free and live a true and honest open life?

When my husband has sex with me, I can only reach a climax by thinking about my lover, and this church husband keeps claiming the glory - that just grieve every bone in my body. I hate it more when I leave my lover's home and come home, and my husband wants me. I smile and let him because I do not want him to be further suspicious.

There is no doubt that my husband is a good Christian, but I did not love him, and nothing has happened in eighteen years to make me love him. He has said that he loves me, and I am sorry he does because I absolutely have none for him. I remain in this bondage only because I made a vow to God!

"I do" has only brought me sadness, tears, failures, grief, pain and endless regrets. My empty life is a clear testimony that I should not have gotten married, at the time I did, or at all.

If I had waited another five or so years; gained more social experiences; reached my goals, then married and this was the result, I don't think I would be so angry because I would have at least made an informed decision. But no one, no one, told me to wait, none.

I know I need to walk away from the relationship with my lover, but I will not give up the only little bit of joy I have.

Against sound doctrine, I force myself to believe that God understands our situation and knows that we deserve each other, in order to feel less or no guilt. We continue to serve Him in our own churches, as officers. No one, not even those who claim to be over-filled with the spirit of discernment, knows my marital pain and the need for God to urgently take my husband to heaven.

Some who read my letters may want to judge and say that I am not a good person, and I can understand that. However, I really wish they would not be too quick to condemn me because many of them have never been in my situation. I still make my husband happy by sacrificing my own happiness, by being around him. He cannot tell anyone that I have ever disrespected or cause him any hurt.

It has not been easy for me to live this double life. My physical heart is literally and constantly nervous especially when my husband and my lover are in the same environment. It has not been easy but what else can I do? I cannot really have the one I want; I cannot marry while my husband is alive, and it is so hard to give up what I true joy and happiness.

Silently Suffering

Compensating

A high level of understanding can be exercised when we see each other through the eyes of each other's sinful nature and frailty. For this reason, we must begin at the beginning, where God created man in His own pure image and likeness and everything was good until man sinned. Adam began good, we began bad!

When mankind sinned, he contaminated the image of God. As a result of this, Genesis 5:3 tells us that, "...Adam ... begat *a son* in ***his own likeness***, after ***his image;*** and called his name Seth." It is clear from this passage that only Adam and Eve were made in the *likeness and image* of God. Each of us has the Adamic *likeness and image*, the contaminated version of God's image.

For this reason, we must treat each other as a bad person striving to do good and not a good person doing bad things; imperfection should not expect perfection from imperfection. While the *born-again* experience brings the carnal nature into subjection it does not eradicate it. The tendency to sin is the contaminated version of God's image, through Adam, and will remain until the righteous is changed from mortal to immortality.

Compensation then is the understanding that your spouse has weaknesses and your responsibility is to pick up the slack. With this commitment fault finding will be replaced by compassion and the need to be strong for your spouse. An example drawn from the home will suffice here, grade your spouse's cooking skills between one and ten, ten being the highest. If you give your spouse 4, then it means you owe your spouse the six lost points. With this obligation in mind, you will never find fault with your spouses' cooking. Your spouse needs you to be ten. Discovering faults and fixing them is always better than finding fault to put your spouse down.

Although chairs are generally made for desks, some chairs will never fit under or around some tables. Before choosing a spouse, you should first know who you are. According to Genesis 2:20, it was after Adam was through naming the animals he discovered there was none suitable for him. Then God made Eve. Both were whole and complete in themselves, but the original plan of God was for His creation to procreate. On his own Adam could not multiply the human specie neither could Eve. When they complimented each other, they fulfilled God's will and had a common, not individual, purpose to live together.

In 1 Peter 3: 1,7 Peter encourages wives to be in subjection to their husbands to win them to the Lord and "...*Likewise*, ye husbands, dwell with them according to knowledge, giving honour unto the wife, as unto the weaker vessel, *and as being heirs together* of the grace of life; that your prayers be not hindered."

The one who brings nothing to make the other person better but expect to be made better should re-examine his/her purpose in the relationship.

An electric bulb will come to life when negative and positive electric wires are properly connected to it. Your relationship will glow when you both compensate and complement each other and others will subsequently be blessed by your union.

Consent

"Marriage is effected by *consent*, freely and knowingly saying *"yes" to all that marriage involves*...when they said their vows, did both partners freely accept and clearly understand the lifelong commitment they were making? ... at that time, *did both partners have the personal capacity to carry out consent, [I Do]?...* Consent must be free and *discerning*...contemporary psychological studies of decision-making shows more sharply how *unconscious motives and situational pressures* can get in the way of freedom and judgment...both partners must have the maturity to establish and sustain a mutually supportive communal relationship..."

(Jeffrey Keefe, O.F.M.Conv.
http://americancatholic.org/newsletters/cu/ac1080.asp)

Almost every institution has entry level requirements and if applicants are not qualified, they are decently rejected. Guardians of the Christian faith have not only disregarded the sanctity of marriage but have turned a blind eye to the effects of broken marriages on parents, children and communities. Not everyone is spiritually, psychologically and socially qualified to be married. Christianity, apparently in the eyes of many, seems to be the only religious institution that has no rules about marriage.

The very *last thing* one wants to do in life, is to get married if one is not ready for a *life-changing* event. Marriage has the potential of retarding or enhancing psychosocial development. It is a world by itself and needs its own space to grow, despite distractions. One must strive to achieve basic life skills and desired goals before *thinking* about marriage. You want to get married after you understand its purpose and your individual roles to achieve that purpose.

For those who choose to become married, the marriage ceremony should be seen as a graduation exercise, in the human maturation process. On the other hand, those who wish to get married but have not completed the basic life span processes should be given an opportunity to do so, outside of marriage.

Mankind and marriage are creations of God, therefore, those who accept Christian marriage cannot look to the laws of men for the meaning and purpose of a Godly union. God created mankind therefore only God can give mankind human rights.

God-centered marriage counselors should endeavor to properly screen each couple to determine if they have the ability to consent to God's marital laws, whether the couple is a Christian or not. This evaluation is necessary because the marriage ceremony is a Christian ceremony and is more than likely performed by a Christian marriage officer. It does not make any sense for that marriage officer, during the ceremony, to passionately warn the couple not to enter marriage inadvisably, yet that same officer did not inform the couple that their marriage also includes consent to God.

Consent also contemplates that the average developmental and life skill disciplines have been achieved by the individual seeking to make a lifelong commitment to a person they will never know.

There is no Biblical mandate that everyone must get married. The fact we all began our lives in singleness means that marriage is an option not a decree. Jesus declared that there are those persons who have chosen to remain single, especially to serve him. "For there are some eunuchs, which were so born from their mother's womb, and there are some eunuchs, which were made eunuchs of men, and there be *eunuchs, which have made themselves eunuchs for the kingdom of heaven's sake. He that is able to receive it, let him receive it"* (Matthew 19:12)

Echoing a similar counsel, Paul said, "I want all of you to be free from worry. An unmarried man worries about how to please the Lord. But a married man has more worries. He must worry about the things of this world, because he wants to please his wife. So, he is pulled in two directions. Unmarried women [widowed/divorced] and women who have never been married worry only about pleasing the Lord, and they keep their bodies and minds pure. But a married woman worries about the things of this world, because she wants to please her husband. What I am saying is for your own good - it isn't to limit your freedom. I want to help you to live right and to love the Lord above all else...it is better to have self-control and to make up your mind not to marry. It is perfectly all right to marry, but it is better not to get married at all." (1 Corinthians 7:32 -35, 37, 38 CEV; emphasis mine)

In the preceding passage, Paul presented singleness as the better option to marriage and classified marriage as worldly. Worldly because pleasing or caring for each other demands *things* of the world which has the strong potential of leading a Christian away from God - marriage can do that!

Like Jesus, the church should present marriage as an option to *singleness* and those who choose not to be married should be given equal respect.

The Christian church needs to do better than some car dealers who sell motor cars but do not provide parts or service. More than any other organization, the church promotes marriages, yet it does not promote counseling for broken hearts. The reason for this is that the church has substituted trained teachers and counselors with preachers and those called prayer-warriors. Then there are some churches that promotes marriage as if it is the next step to God's salvation plan.

Someone may ask if the devil has been attacking marriages and families? Maybe, maybe not. What is very clear is that if six-year-old children are given driver's licenses to drive tractor-trailers and fatal accidents have increased, one cannot blame the road.

The fact is, the Christian 'born again' experience is a spiritual matter that prepares a person to go to heaven. It does not rehabilitate a person who is socially dysfunctional; it does not convert people into marriage materials and it certainly does not guarantee a successful marriage.

Jeffrey Keefe lists three "Emotional problems that could make a person incapable to consent:

> ***Personality Disorder*** - ingrained maladaptive patterns of behavior, usually with roots in early life, and often evident by adolescence.

> ***Psychoses*** - the disintegrative mental illness such as schizophrenia and manic depression.

> ***Insecurity*** - lack of trust; belief that no one can be true to them."

Marriage is a great institution and everyone who seeks to enter it must be mature and ready to live by its rules, as set by God.

Proper pre-marital counseling is also vital as it seeks to identify ones' level of readiness and essential skills to cope with marital challenges.

What an individual brings, socially, academically, financially and psychologically into the other person's life is most important for self-actualization and validation. Marriage cannot only be about love. It should include one's capacity, ability and readiness to help the other reach desired goals and sustain those that have been achieved.

Marriage is not the time to be building traits nor is counseling the time to be telling the couple how to be a good husband and wife. Amongst the many other social and academic disciplines, at this point, the counselor should be looking for

- the traits of awareness and insightfulness at the mental level;

- various attitudes at the vital level;

- and physical makeup and well-being at the physical level.

The counselor must be open and honest to tell the couple what observable characteristics are being manifested and if he/she believes the couple is mature to consent to the substance of Christian marriage vows.

In marriage, there is no right or wrong person for God will not make a perfect gift out of another person to please an imperfect you. Sin has truly impaired a person's ability to see perfectly and yet that same impaired vision must be used to make such lifelong decision.

Jesus has given clear instructions, that if Christians wish to marry their choice must be from the practicing Christian community. But one should not believe that this command guarantees a perfect choice for Jesus, in Matthew 13:24 -30, also described the pool of Christians from which to choose as *Wheat and Tares*! You can marry a devil out of any Holy Ghost filled church and would not know what you have until time exposes his or her true character.

Traits defines character, it is the sum total of an individual's disposition and marriage interlock these unchangeable traits. For this reason, you should be intimate with some level of psychology or common sense. For example, if your significant other is always apologizing for behavioral problems and you believe the promises to change after marriage, you would be stupid because marriage is not a mental health clinic. People with special needs sometimes use marriage, to you, as the means to escape or meet such needs.

Consent will be constantly challenged by each other's opinion, choices and decisions. This is where the mind engages maturation to prevent, mitigate or handle conflicts. Of course, the side effect of this constant pounding, of character, may even resurrect dormant traits that were earlier suppressed.

The one who is ready to consent will engage the skills learnt through varied experiences and maturation to reasonably handle predictable and unpredictable situations.

One of the greatest privileges that God has given to mankind is marriage. It gives the permission for intimate recreation as well as the power to procreate - give life. Its beauty and magnificent glory can be experienced, by Christians or non-Christians, when it is engaged for its God given goals. It can be used to validate each other, improve families and communities. It is a great responsibility.

It is my hope that the information in this book will:

1. Help the couple to examine their decision and choice to be married.

2. Help the couple to objectively examine each other.

3. Help the couple to evaluate each other's ability to communicate socially, emotionally, spiritually, financially, academically and psychologically.

4. Help the couple to examine their level of maturity and each other's readiness to face the unpredictable consequences of a shared life.

5. Help the couple to understand and accept the meaning of Christian Marriage and the capacity to carry out consent.

6. Help the counselor to develop a sound understanding, opinion and profile of the couple.

Like medicine interacting with ones' body chemistry, relationships and marriages have emotional, social, spiritual and psychological side effects, *so face the facts and forget fictions* – marriage has permanent lifelong consequences.

Marriage, Divorce, Remarriage

"...While her husband liveth, she be married to another man, she shall be called an adulteress..." (Romans 7:3)

As sole guardians and perpetrators of the laws, the Pharisees knew what Jesus taught about marriage, divorce and remarriage. For this reason, they wanted to tempt Him to change what His teaching has always been, as well as to put Him in contempt with the alleged teachings of Moses. The teachings of Jesus were in contention with that of the Pharisees, for this they had to do something about Jesus.

Amidst their many obvious atrocities the Pharisees still performed their ritualistic form of godliness. But God would have already spoken,

"And this have ye done again, covering the altar of the Lord with tears, with weeping, and with crying out, ...the Lord hath been witness between thee and the wife of thy youth, against whom thou hast dealt treacherously yet is she thy companion, and the wife of thy **covenant**. And did not he make one? Yet had he the residue of the spirit. And wherefore one? That he might seek a godly seed. Therefore, take heed to your spirit, and let none deal treacherously against the wife of his youth. **For the Lord, the God of Israel, saith that he hateth putting away** (divorce), for one covereth violence with his garment, saith the Lord of hosts therefore take heed to your spirit, that ye deal not treacherously." (Malachi 2:13-16)

The Pharisees' discontent was about remarriage, how to get it done while a husband or wife was still alive. Divorce then, would be the only doorway, to remarriage, and Jesus was taking away that key they said Moses gave them.

In Matthew chapter 19:3, the Pharisees began their temptation with, "Is it **lawful** for a man to put away his wife for **every cause**?" This question establishes the context and subject for the ensuing discourse, which may be broken into two:

(1) is divorce *lawful?*

(2) is divorce lawful for *every cause?*

In response to the first part of their challenge Jesus appealed to what He knew they knew, "Have ye not read that He who made them at the beginning made them male and female. And said, for this cause shall a man leave mother and father and shall cleave to his wife, and they twain shall be one flesh? Wherefore, they are no more twain, but one flesh." Later He warned, "What therefore God hath joined together, let not man put asunder." (Mat. 19: 7)

Their first attempt failed so they next introduced their crown witness, Moses. [If it were not lawful] "Why did Moses then command to give her a writing of divorcement, and to put her away?" (Matthew 19:4-6)

Continuing His response, Jesus told them that Moses gave them that regulation because their forefathers were spiritually hardened against the will of God. "Moses, because of the hardness of your hearts, suffered you to put away your wives, but from the beginning it was not so." (Matthew 19:8) Here Jesus informed them that Moses did not institute divorce and remarriage but regulated what their fathers did.

Divorce then, was born out of sin which hardened their hearts against the known will of God. It is for this reason Jesus said, *from the beginning it was not so* – **divorce is not in God's marital institution**! If God hates divorce, which originated out of the hardness of man's heart, why would He endorse it? Contextually, Jesus was simply clarifying Moses' regulation which they were abusing.

Attending to the second part of their test, Jesus explained that Moses did not say for every reason, "And I say unto you [repeating the Mosaic reason], whosoever shall put away his wife, except it be for *fornication*, and shall marry another, [that married man] committeth adultery, and whoso marrieth her which is put away doth commit adultery."

This was the Mosaic regulation,

"When a man hath taken a wife, and married her, and it come to pass that she finds no favour in his eyes, because he hath found some uncleanness in her: then let him write her a bill of divorcement, and give it in her hand, and send her out of his house. When she is departed out of his house, she may go and be another man's wife. If the latter husband hate her, and write her a bill of divorcement, and giveth it in her hand, and sendeth her out of his house; or if the latter husband die, which took her to be his wife; former husband, which sent her away, may not take her again to be his wife, after that she is defiled; for that is abomination before the LORD: and thou shalt not cause the land to sin, which the LORD thy God giveth thee for an inheritance." (Deuteronomy 24:1-4)

Moses did not say for every reason but for uncleanness, *sexual intercourse **before** marriage*. In explaining this Mosaic exception Jesus uses the words *fornication* and *adultery* in the same sentence, two different things. A married person does not commit fornication! So, Jesus is further explaining to them what Moses said and meant. Here is Moses again,

(1) "If any man takes a wife, and go in unto her, and hate her. And give occasions of speech against her, and bring up an evil name upon her, and say, I took this woman, and when I came to her, I found her not a *maid* [virgin].

(2) Then shall the father of the damsel, and her mother, take and bring forth the tokens of the damsel's virginity unto the elders of the city in the gate.

(3) And the damsel's father shall say unto the elders, I gave my daughter unto this man to wife, and he hateth her. And, lo, he hath given occasions of speech against her, saying, I found not thy daughter a maid, and yet these are the tokens of my daughter's virginity.

(4) And they shall spread the cloth before the elders of the city. And the elders of that city shall take that man and chastise him.

(5) And they shall amerce him in an hundred shekels of silver, and give them unto the father of the damsel, because he hath brought up an evil name upon a virgin of Israel, and she shall be his wife; *he may not put her away all his days*.

(6) But if this thing be true, and the tokens of virginity be not found for the damsel. Then they shall bring out the damsel to the door of her father's house, and the men of her city shall stone her with stones that she die: because she hath wrought folly in Israel, to play the whore in her father's house.

(7) So shalt thou put evil away from among you." (Deuteronomy 22:13 -21)

Clearly, in the Mosaic regulation, if *fornication* was **not** committed then there was no reason to even contemplate divorce. But, if she was given, to man, as a virgin and was not then he had grounds to contemplate divorce.

In Deuteronomy 24, Moses required the first husband to give his wife a divorce document to protect her and to prove to her next husband that she did not lose her virginity as a result of harlotry. With this information a man may choose to marry that divorced woman.

Two things must be noted in the Mosaic regulation, it:

1. did not allow reconciliation, by the first husband

2. did not recognize adultery, when a man marries a divorced woman

The highly debated and reiterated *exception,* in Matthew 19:9, by today's church, was only addressing the grounds for divorce, not remarriage. It is clear that adultery was committed when a person's spouse was still alive and he or she marries again. According to Jesus, divorce does not cancel a marriage and that is why remarriage is adultery.

Jesus said that from the beginning there was no *exception* and He was not, now, giving one to satisfy their already hardened hearts. They asked Him if it was lawful and why Moses allowed it. Jesus clarified what Moses meant and reminded them that it was their sinful hearts that forced Moses to regulate their practice. This regulation also included a bill that gave civil rights and protection to women.

Moses found this was necessary because women could be stoned to death for harlotry. Divorce then, was contestable by the woman and was not for every cause. Joseph, like the disciples, was also exposed to the Pharisaic teaching and punishment about an adulterous woman. Yet when he found out Mary was pregnant, he intended to protect her by putting her away privately.

"Then Joseph her husband, being a just man, and not willing to make her a public example [stoning her to death], was minded to put her away privately. But while he thought on these things, behold, the angel of the Lord appeared unto him in a dream, saying, Joseph, thou son of David, fear not to take unto thee Mary thy wife: for that which is conceived in her is of the Holy Ghost…Joseph, being raised from sleep, did as the angel of the Lord had bidden him, and took unto him his wife." (Matthew 1: 19, 20, 24)

When Jesus' disciples understood His response, they, not the Pharisees, blurted out, "If the case of the man be so with his wife it is not good to marry [in the first place]. But he said unto them, all men cannot receive this saying, save they to whom it is given." (Matthew 19:10, 11) In other words, Jesus' statement would be offensive to those who were not willing to obey Him.

The Pharisees had asked if it was lawful to divorce but Jesus captured the moment to highlight:

(1) Moses said that divorce *could* happen for this cause.

(2) Jesus said that from the beginning there was no divorce but because of the hardness of their minds Moses imposed a regulation.

(3) Jesus said that remarriage is what constituted adultery; an adulterous state of being.

These were the points which aroused the interest of the disciples. Now, to emphasize the seriousness of His points, Jesus continued, "There are some eunuchs, who were so born [impotent] from their mother's womb, and there are some eunuchs, who were made eunuchs of men [castrated, emphasis added] *and there be eunuchs, which have made themselves eunuchs* [remained unmarried] *for the kingdom of heaven's sake*. He that is able to receive it [the teaching on divorce and remarriage], let him receive it." (Matthew 19:3-12)

It was Jesus' irritating truth that compelled the disciples to seek clarification, for they too trusted and shared the belief of the religious elite. They understood Jesus' response to mean that they were not permitted to remarry. For this reason, they responded, "*If the case of the man be so with his wife, it is good not to marry* [in the first place]."

Some scholars, who have vandalized the substance of scriptural truth, loosely use the word fornication to mean sexual unfaithfulness *after* marriage, to justify reasons for divorce and remarriage.

Adultery was in two forms, when:

1. there is sexual unfaithfulness *after* marriage

2. one marries a divorced person

Moses, Jesus and Paul agreed that fornication has to be **before** marriage. Here is Paul's recommendation, "…To avoid *fornication*, let every man have his own wife, and let every woman have her own husband." (1 Corinthians 7:2)

Uncleanness and fornication both speak to sexual misconduct *before* marriage. There are at least four forms of the Greek words used in English to mean fornication (*Strong's Exhaustive Concordance*):

(1) *porneia* – harlotry, adultery, incest.

(2) *porneuo* – unlawful lust.

(3) *pornay* – a female harlot, whore.

(4) *pornos* – to sell; a male prostitute, whore.

The two forms of the Hebrew word used to mean uncleanness are:

(1) *ervaw* – nudity, disgrace, blemish.

(2) *awraw* – bare, empty, pour out, demolish, leave destitute, discover, make naked, spread self, uncover.

The apostle Paul, who learnt through special revelation from Jesus, also understood the sacredness of the marriage union. "Art thou bound unto a wife? *Seek* [enquire/endeavor] not to be loosed [Greek *losis* - divorce]. Art thou loosed from a wife? Seek not a wife." (1 Corinthians 7:27) Paul observes that there is a bond, in marriage which one should not *endeavor* to break.

According to Exodus 19:1, Israel reached Sinai three months after the left Egypt. So, it was not long after they left Egypt that God would have spoken to them about the ways of the Egyptians and Canaanites. The practice preceded the command. Moses would have written his response about their misbehavior during their journey between Mount Sinai, where he received the commands and Mount Nebo, where he died. Therefore, the hardness of man's heart was just after they were given the command, "Thou shalt not commit adultery...thou shalt not covet thy neighbour's wife." (Ex. 20:14, 16)

They immediately hardened their hearts, against God, and continued the practice they learnt in Egypt. They were in rebellion.

As a result of what Canaan did to his grandfather, Genesis 9:21 - 25, Canaan was cursed. Therefore, the Israelites were also warned against the sexual practices of the Egyptians and Canaanites, but the older Israelites rebelled and passed these practices over to their children.

"And the Lord spake unto Moses, saying. Speak unto the children of Israel, and say unto them, I am the Lord your God. After the doings of the land of Egypt, wherein ye dwelt, shall ye not do: and after the doings of the land of Canaan, whither I bring you, shall ye not do neither shall ye walk in their ordinances...Moreover, thou shalt not lie carnally with thy neighbor's wife, to defile thyself with her." (Lev. 18:1-3, 20)

Divorce could not be of the Lord for whenever or wherever He referred to the practice it was used in a derogatory way or in mockery of Israel's lifestyle. For example, in Jeremiah chapter 3 the Lord used the Mosaic regulation to warn Judah because Israel had not listened to Him.

"...When for all the causes whereby backsliding Israel committed adultery, I had put her away, and given her a bill of divorce...Turn, O backsliding children, saith the LORD; for I am married unto you: and I will take you one of a city, and two of a family, and I will bring you to Zion." (Jeremiah 3: 8, 14)

With harsh sarcasm, the Lord said He had given the Israelites His Mosaic bill-of-divorce because they were behaving like prostitutes. But His genuine encouragement was for her reconciliation.

The Pharisees, a splinter group from the internal Maccabean rivalry *(2003, Robert H. Gundry, A Survey of the New Testament, p. 63, Zondervan, Grand Rapids),* were never appointed or anointed by God. They, however, positioned themselves, throughout the New Testament, as chief interpreters and enforcers of the laws. These same Pharisees Jesus said, "...Trusted in themselves that they were righteous, and despised others." (Luke 18:9) They were the ones who wanted to kill Jesus, "Then from that day forth they took counsel together to put him to death." (John 11:53)

In an attempt to disinfect Israel's marital misbehavior, Moses initiated many regulations. In two of them he declared that a man who rapes a woman had to marry her and the Priests were told that they should not marry a divorced woman.

"If a man find a damsel that is a virgin, which is not betrothed, and lay hold on her, and lie with her, and they be found; the man that lay with her shall give unto the damsel's father fifty shekels of silver, and she shall be his wife; because he hath humbled her, he may not put her away *all his days...* And the LORD said unto Moses, Speak unto the priests the sons of Aaron, and say unto them,...They shall not take a wife that is a whore, or profane; *neither shall they take a woman put away from her husband*: for he is holy unto his God" (Deuteronomy 22:28,29; Leviticus 21:1,7)

God not only told Israel to leave the Egyptians' way of life but also warned them not to take up the ways of the Canaanites. Divorce and remarriage were of the Egyptians and Canaanites. Would God have warned His people against divorce and remarriage then later tell them it was okay?

When Matthew chapter 5 is brought into evidence, it is further observed that Jesus was explaining *when* adultery was committed, "Ye have heard that it was said by them of old time, Thou shalt not commit adultery. But I say unto you, that ***whosoever looketh on a woman to lust after her hath committed adultery*** **with her already in his heart.**" (Matthew 5: 27, 28)

The righteousness of the Pharisee limited adultery to a physical act. But, according to Jesus, lusting is a sexual sin, of the heart, and can be classified as adultery or fornication.

The Pharisees, however, were concerned with the grounds for divorce, but Jesus wanted them to be concerned about the nature of marriage.

After Jesus left the Pharisees, in the book of Matthew, Mark recorded that the disciples were still not convinced, so, "In the house His disciples asked him **again** of the same matter. [And again, Jesus said] Whomsoever shall put away his wife and marry, commit adultery against her. [Then He added a unique statement] And *if a woman shall put away her husband* and be married to another she committeth adultery." (Mark 10: 10-12) Notice, Jesus was not explaining any conditions or causes, in the house. He did that already, now he was teaching His disciples the sacredness and permanency of Marriage.

In another instance, according to John, the dissatisfied Pharisees again waited for another occasion to tempt Jesus. But this time they went with the Scribes and a human exhibit.

"Jesus went unto the mount of Olives. And early in the morning he came again into the temple, and all the people came unto him and he sat down and taught them. And the scribes and Pharisees brought unto him a woman taken in adultery and when they had set her in the midst.

They say unto him, Master, this woman was taken in adultery, in the very act. Now Moses in the law commanded us, that such should be stoned but what sayest thou? **This they said, tempting him, that they might have to accuse him.** But Jesus stooped down, and with his finger wrote on the ground, as though he heard them not. So, when they continued asking him, he lifted up himself, and said unto them, he that is without sin among you, let him first cast a stone at her.

And again, he stooped down, and wrote on the ground. And they which heard it, being convicted by their own conscience, went out one by one, beginning at the eldest, even unto the last, and Jesus was left alone, and the woman standing in the midst. When Jesus had lifted up himself, and saw none but the woman, he said unto her, Woman, where are those thine accusers? Hath no man condemned thee? She said, no man, Lord. And Jesus said unto her, neither do I condemn thee go, and sin no more. Then spake Jesus again unto them, saying, I am the light of the world he that followeth me shall not walk in darkness, but shall have the light of life. The Pharisees therefore said unto him, Thou bearest record of thyself *thy record is not true."* (John 8:1-13)

Although they appealed to the law of Moses, Jesus did not bother to repeat what Moses said and meant. What He did was:

(1) Wrote something on the ground

(2) Petitioned their conscience, "he that is without sin among you, let him first cast a stone at her." The reason for saying this is that Moses had also said that it is the *"sinless* witness" who must *first* stone the accused, "The hands of the witnesses shall be first upon him to put him to death, and afterward the hands of all the people..." (Deuteronomy 17:7)

(3) Told them He was Life and they should follow Him (instead of the law).

(4) Told them that the Devil was their father.

Not to be dissuaded by their failure, they then attacked His authority. It is at this time Jesus said,

"Ye are of your father the devil, and the lusts of your father ye will do. He was a murderer from the beginning, and abode not in the truth, because there is no truth in him. When he speaketh a lie, he speaketh of his own for he is a liar, and the father of it. And because **I tell you the truth, ye believe me not**. Which of you convinceth me of sin? And if I say the truth, why do ye not believe me? **He that is of God heareth God's words** ye therefore hear them not, because ye are not of God." (John 8:41-47)

In Matthew's account, Jesus repeated that if the divorced person remarries, that person commits adultery. Divorce, then, did not and cannot dissolve a marriage, "What God has joined together let no man put asunder." Only death can end a marriage. No man has the authority or ability to undo those whom God has united.

Modern courts recognize that only death can end a marriage. For this reason, divorce decrees are phrased "[Divorce]…Shall take effect **as if the former spouse had died** on the date on which the marriage is dissolved…" (*In The High Court of Justice, Principal Registry of the Family Division – section 18A of the Wills Act 1837*)

This artificial death, is to superimpose itself on the respondent *'as if the former had died.'* This evidence proves that divorce courts accepts death as the only reason to end what God has joined together. Further, the declaration *as if the former had died* is supposed to mean that the courts did not put asunder what had been joined – it was caused by death.

In their book, *The Marriage Bed,* Paul and Lori wrote,

> 'First, we need to understand that **marriage is a covenant, not a contract**. A contract can have loopholes, can be broken by mutual agreement, and usually expires or must be renewed after a specified time. A covenant is very different - it is intended to continue as long as those who have entered into it are alive, it cannot be broken by mutual agreement, and there are no loopholes. In days of old, violating the bounds of a covenant resulted in death. This was the

punishment for adultery given to the Jews by God. The death of the one who had broken the covenant left no doubt that the covenant had ended, and the person who was still alive was no longer bound by the covenant."

Endorsing and continuing Jesus' teaching, Paul said, "Unto the married I command, **yet not I but the Lord**, let not the wife depart from her husband. The wife is bound by the law as long as her husband liveth, but if her husband be dead, she is at liberty to be married to whom she will, only in the Lord [a Christian]." However, where there is separation, "Let her remain unmarried, or be reconciled to her husband, and let not the husband put away his wife." (1 Corinthians 7:10, 11, 39)

"For the woman which hath a husband is bound by the law to her husband so long as he liveth, but if the husband be dead, she is loosed from the law of her husband. So then if, *while her husband liveth, she be married to another man, she shall be called an adulteress* but if her husband be dead, she is free from that law so that she is no adulteress, though she be married to another man." (Romans 7:2,3) Consistently with Jesus, Paul here says that adultery is committed when any of the married persons remarry while the other is still alive.

The patriarchal community used the *Mosaic Marriage Regulation* to recycle their wives. One can therefore understand why the Samaritan woman honestly confessed to Jesus that she had no husband, "...Thou hast well said, I have no husband, for thou hast had five husbands and he whom thou now hast is not thy husband, in that saidst thou truly." (John 4:17, 18)

The fact that Jesus used the legal term "husband" confirms the fact that she was not a harlot. The Godly institution only recognize the first husband therefore, the one that was with her was not hers. Knowing how abusive the Mosaic Marriage Regulation had become, Jesus did not have any reason to condemn the woman caught in adultery, John 8:1-11, the woman of Samaria or any other abused woman.

Paul explained to the Corinthians that if there was a situation that may cause one party to depart, both should remain separated for life or be reconciled to each other. Further, in his recommendation to Timothy, about women who were qualified to be widows, he said that a widow should have been the wife of only one man. She should not have had an ex-husband. "Let not a widow be taken into the number under threescore years old, having been the wife of one man...A bishop then must be blameless, the husband of one wife..." (1 Timothy 5:9; 3:2)

Although prominent Bible characters like Abraham, David and Solomon had more than one wife, it must be noted that none was approved by God. Polygamy was not a prescribed way of life, so it is obvious that Paul was not talking about multiple spouses.

After presenting what the Lord revealed to him, Paul said, "To the rest I speak not the Lord...if the unbelieving depart, let him depart. A brother or a sister is not under bondage in such cases but God hath called us to peace." (1 Corinthians 7:15)

Many have interpreted the Pauline's phrase *not under bondage* to mean that there is an innocent party who is free to remarry. But Paul did not say that. The phrase does not constitute nor contemplates remarriage. Also, the passage does not seek to identify modern scholar's **innocent party,** there is no such terminology in the Bible. The marital issue in the passage was relative to religious differences, not marital unfaithfulness.

Further, Paul could not be saying that an individual, who was separated, **ought to seek reconciliation** and at the same time, in the same context, also be saying that the said individual **may divorce and or remarry**.

Bondage (Greek, *douloo* - to enslave; a servant) must mean marital obligations - the brother or sister was not to be held responsible for the unbeliever's liabilities.

The fact is, in the patriarchal custom, a girl was taken care of by her father, brother, or her husband. In this context, wives were provided for by their husbands. No other man was responsible for her food, clothing and shelter. In this New Testament sense, a brother or sister had no obligations to the one who leaves.

Another point to note is that Paul's statement "let him depart*"* speaks to *separation* and not a Mosaic *putting away* – divorce. The condition for this separation, Paul said, was motivated by religious differences, and not any of the Mosaic causes.

Both Moses' and Paul were addressing two different people about two different issues. Paul was not repeating nor clarifying anything Moses said, but was re-enforcing the principles of Jesus.

While Moses intent was to put order to disorder, Paul's intent was for the couple to work out their differences. If this was not achieved, then they were free to be separated for the sake of peace and remain unmarried.

The Pharisees, who wounded the religious structure of the Jewish society, were the ones who taught that it was right to love brethren and hate the enemy; they were the ones who were challenging Jesus about divorce and remarriage, they did not forgive.

On the lesson of forgiveness Jesus said,

"Ye have heard that it hath been said, thou shalt love thy neighbour, and hate thine enemy. But I say unto you, Love your enemies, bless them that curse you, do good to them that hate you, and pray for them which despitefully use you, and persecute you that ye may be the children of your Father which is in heaven. For he maketh his sun to rise on the evil and on the good, and sendeth rain on the just and on the unjust. For if ye love them which love you, what reward have ye? Do not even the publicans the same? And if ye salute your brethren only, what do ye more than others? Do not even the publicans so? Be ye therefore perfect, even as your Father which is in heaven is perfect." (Matthew 5: 43-48)

Although a Christian spouse may be separated, maliciousness or hatred should not be in his/her heart, for one is expected to love. Especially at the Lord 's Supper, the believers' heart must be worthy to commune with the Lord. This requirement is strongly implied in Jesus' statement, "Therefore if thou bring thy gift to the altar, and there rememberest that thy brother ought against thee. Leave there thy gift before the altar, and go thy way, first be reconciled to thy brother, and then come and offer thy gift." (Matthew 5: 23, 24)

God *is* Love and it is therefore impossible to truly love, if God is absent from one's heart. Separation should not breed hatred.

It was an easy thing for the Pharisees to love their brethren but an impossible task to love their enemies. Jesus' encouragement was that, just as He allows the undeserving sinner to enjoy His sun and rain, His children should be, "Perfect [in love], even as your Father which is in heaven is perfect." For anyone to be a child of God his righteousness must exceed the righteousness of the Pharisee.

Paul's final lesson on the issue is to be found in the statement, "Husbands love your wives as Christ loved the church and gave Himself up for her." (Ephesians 5:25) The marital life can only be lived according to the example of love taught and demonstrated by Jesus. Consider all that mankind had done to Him and yet He still loves them.

When things were not going right, and the church separated herself, from God, He waited for her to be reconciled to Him. On one occasion Hosea was asked to marry a prostitute to teach God's people that although they divorced Him, He was still waiting for them to reconcile with Him.

Peter had gone to Jesus and asked, "Lord, how oft shall my brother sin [offend] against me, and I forgive him? Till seven times? Jesus saith unto him, I say not unto thee, until seven times but, until seventy times seven" (Matthew 18: 21, 22). Jesus gave up His life for a bride - the church, who betrayed, persecuted, lied, and crucified Him. Yet, while they were crucifying Him, He was praying for their forgiveness.

How many times then should a spouse forgive the other, the one vowed to be loved, for better or worse and until death? Christians have a responsibility to teach the world what true forgiveness and reconciliation means, putting an end to divorce and remarriage.

The intent of the Pharisee's temptation was to destroy and substitute God's sacred institution for what the *hardness of the heart desired.* Jesus directed the Pharisees to the scripture – *it is written...from beginning.*

Divorce, with the intent to remarry, is an absolute disregard to the command of the Lord, "What God has joined together, let no man put asunder."

Personal Comments

The longer you take to get married the longer you stay married

The question of the unequally yoked "Marriages."

Be ye not unequally yoked together with **unbelievers** for what fellowship hath *righteousness with unrighteousness?* and *what communion hath light with darkness?* And what concord hath Christ with Belial? or *what part hath he that believeth with an infidel?* And what agreement hath the temple of God with idols? for ye are the temple of the living God; as God hath said, I will dwell in them, and walk in *them;* and I will be their God, and they shall be my people. **Come out from among them, and be ye separate, saith the Lord, and touch not the unclean *thing;* and I will receive you**,. And will be a Father unto you, and ye shall be my sons and daughters, saith the Lord Almighty." (2 Corinthians 6:14-18)

I have had to rethink this passage multiple times and have confidently concluded that the context has nothing to do with marriage but does not exclude marriages. According to verses 3 and 4, ibid, *"**Giving no offence in anything, that the ministry be not blamed. But in all things approving ourselves as the ministers of God**…"* That is it, the context is relationships, **_any_** contracted relationship (agreement to yoke especially with sinners).

In this instance Paul's recommendation is for the righteous; the light; the believer; the temple of God; God's people to come out from among *them*. But them who? Those of the faith (1 Cor. 5:9-13) and the heathen who can cause you to be a disgrace to the ministry and bring the name of God into disrepute.

The phrase "unequally yoked" have been incorrectly used for decades to restrain Christians from marrying an unsaved person (ideally a Christian should marry a Christian).

The inconsistent meaning of unequally yoked does show up our hypocrisy when we recommend a couple to get married because one of the two has become a Christian. Is this not also unequally yoked together with an unbeliever, sanctioned by the Pastor? Yes. Unequally yoked does not have one meaning for the Christian who falls in love with an unsaved and another meaning for new born Christian marrying a spouse of many years. The fact is, many of our most God-fearing and faithful married congregants have unsaved spouses!

In addressing a marital relationship between the saved and the unsaved Peter said, "Likewise, ye wives, *be* in subjection to your own husbands; that, if any obey not the word, they also may without the word be won by the conversation of the wives…Likewise, ye husbands, dwell with *them* according to knowledge, giving honour unto the wife, as unto the weaker vessel, and as being heirs together of the grace of life; that your prayers be not hindered." (1 Peter 3:1,7)

In the same breath Paul said, "If any brother hath a wife that believeth not, and she be pleased to dwell with him, let him not put her away. And the woman which hath an husband that believeth not, and if he be pleased to dwell with her, let her not leave him. For the unbelieving husband is sanctified by the wife, and the unbelieving wife is sanctified by the husband..." (1 Cor. 7: 13, 14)

The phrase unequally yoked is not synonymous with marriage but refers to Christians having a bond relationship with the unsaved, which has the potential to bring disrepute to God and Christianity.

Marriages not Sanction by God:

The debate on divorce and remarriage should not be rooted in Jesus' explanation of the Mosaic *exception* but in Jesus' statement, "what God has joined together, let no man put asunder." (Matthew 19:6b)

The statement clearly implies that there are marriages that God does not endorse, and if so, then these can be broken.

However, what God has joined or not joined, becomes very subjective as there is no Biblical description for this. Marriage ceremonies are determined by culture which changes with people and time. An appreciation for which marriage is sanctioned by God may comes from clear Biblical evidence, marriage customs and manners and New Testament marital statements.

Such marriages are:

1. Same sex marriages

For the wrath of God is revealed from heaven against all ungodliness and unrighteousness of men, who hold the truth in unrighteousness;...Because that, when they knew God, they glorified *him* not as God, neither were thankful; but became vain in their imaginations, and their foolish heart was darkened...Wherefore God also gave them up to uncleanness through the lusts of their own hearts, to dishonour their own bodies between themselves:...For this cause God gave them up unto vile affections: for even their women did change the natural use into that which is against nature. And likewise, also the men, leaving the natural use of the woman, burned in their lust one toward another; men with men working that which is unseemly, and receiving in themselves that recompence of their error which was meet. Even as they did not like to retain God in *their* knowledge, God gave them over to a reprobate mind, to do those things which are not convenient."

(Romans 1:18, 21,24,26 -28)

2. *Marriages not done in Jesus' name*

And whatsoever ye do in word or deed, *do* all in the name of the Lord Jesus, giving thanks to God and the Father by him." (Colossians 3:17)

3. Atheist

It would be a mockery if an atheist requests a Christian marriage. The person who does not believe that there is a God equally cannot believe that marriage is an institution of God. For this reason, such a person cannot make a marriage vow to God.

4. Business Marriages

A contractual marriage for the purpose of personal goal, especially to legally stay in a country. These marriages are self-defined, not real, and are not of God.

Another form of business marriage is when one party have a debilitating condition (especially medical, and financial) decides to marry to personally benefit from the other, without disclosing the condition.

5. Frivolous Marriages

"For as in the days that were before the flood they were eating and drinking, marrying and giving in marriage until the day that Noe entered into the ark." (Matthew 24:38)

This lighthearted type of marriage is usually done because it can be done or merely to sometimes please one of the parties. While these marriages are legal, they are not approved by God.

What about the person who has been divorced or intends to do so? From the discourses of Moses, Jesus and Paul, while divorce is an act displeasing to God, it is only at remarriage that adultery is committed.

Remarriage was the problem. Listen to Jesus' commentary on what Moses said, "And I say unto you, Whosoever shall put away his wife, except *it be* for fornication (sexual intercourse *before* marriage), and shall marry another, committeth adultery and whoso marrieth her which is put away doth commit adultery." (Matthew 19:9)

Now listen to Paul, "So then if, while *her* husband liveth, she be married to another man, she shall be called an adulteress, but if her husband be dead, she is free from that law; so that she is no adulteress, though she be married to another man...But if the *unbelieving* depart, **let him depart**. A brother or a sister is not under bondage in such *cases:* but God hath called us to peace." (**Romans 7:3;** 1 Corinthians 7:15)

According to Jesus, adultery happens at **remarriage and makes the individual an adulterer or adulteress. The Pharisees wanted to use divorce as a doorway for remarriage but Paul's recommendation for separation was to settle religious issues.**

Divorce nor remarriage cannot dissolve a marriage union, only death. Remarriage is what constitutes adultery, while one's spouse is alive.

There are two aspects to marriage:

1. The **civil signing** is that legislative aspect by which the brides' family name is amended. This exercise has nothing to do with God.

2. The **religious** aspect takes the form of a *vow to God* and sexual intercourse by the couple. It is at sexual intercourse that the man and the woman become *one flesh*.

Both aspects are most evident in many marriage ceremonies when there is (1) a vow and (2) a signing. For this reason, the civil courts can only grant a civil divorce - the signing- but cannot release the parties of their vows to God.

A civil divorce is most relevant and when necessary should be employed to protect oneself against liabilities, abuse and other demanding reasons. This is synonymous to the separation recommended by Paul.

The clear instruction from Paul is, "Be ye not unequally yoked together with unbelievers..." (2 Corinthians 6:14) But in a community that is not govern by theocracy there will be marriages but are all *Christian* marriages?

As we seek to define Christian marriages let us first consider the difference between Christianity and Practicing Christian:

Christianity is the name of the religion started by Jesus. In the first century it was hijacked and captured by Roman Catholicism. Consequently,

- A baptismal name, called a Christian name, is given at baptism or at dedication services.

- Living in the Roman territory made the individual a Christian, rather than confession of sins and acceptance of Jesus.

- If you are not a Hindu, Buddhist, Atheist, Muslim etc., you are classified as a Christian.

In the past, Government and legal documents had sections labeled as *Christian Name*, but religious tolerance and insult to other religion has now changed those sections to *"Given or Family Name."*

A practicing Christian is one who has repented of sins and have accepted Jesus as Lord and Savior.

In light of the 2 Corinthians 6:14, it is pertinent to discuss what makes a marriage a Christian marriage:

i. A sinner conducting a marriage between two Christians, in Jesus' name?

ii. A Christian conducting a marriage between two sinners, in Jesus' name?

iii. A Christian conducting a marriage between two sinners who believes in Jesus?

iv. A Christian conducting a marriage between two practicing Christians?

v.   A marriage where a vow is made by the couple to God?

In contrast to Christianity, a Muslim cleric would never marry a non-Muslim to a Muslim nor would he perform a wedding for a Christian couple. Christianity **appears** to be the only religion that allows its adherents to marry as they will.

George Barna, president and founder of Barna Research Group, commented, "*While it may be alarming to discover that born again Christians are more likely than others to experience a divorce, that pattern has been in place for quite some time…*"

(http://www.religioustolerance.org/chr_dira.htm)

If the Barna's findings is correct, the high rate of divorce amongst Christians is a sad reflection of the respect given this Godly institution and God's prescriptive command, *What God has put Let no man put asunder.*

The Counseling Session

Preparation for Counseling:

Dating - simple setting a date and time with activities with a person. At this point you may date different persons without making commitments; nothing suggestive must be manifested. To make a promise, commitment or to be suggestive, at this time, may constitute flirting.

Steady Dating - mature commitment is made at this time. Casual dating others can still occur but if you or your spouse is uncomfortable with either person, casually going out with others then your relation-ship is already at risk.

Courting - at this time one is far more comfortable dating the significant other and may now make one's intention public. You are an individual; healthy dating is ok.

Counseling - this is where an experienced or professional person is invited to assist you in the final part of the decision-making process, pre-marital counseling.

The Counseling Team:

1. *Chief* - interview couple; completes main counseling; meet with the counseling team; approve or disapprove marriage. Make referral when necessary

2. **Legal Personnel** - discuss the relationship of current individual assets, titles, life insurance, family-ties to assets and or other future assets.

3. *Medical Personnel* - evaluate health status and determine if there is the presence of heredity issues. For example, if Sickle Cell is present the Doctor will discuss its implication on the couple's finance; the child's future and how it may dictate or limit the type of job that one can take.

4. *Psychologist* - search for trauma; explore, assess and prepare report on the mental health of the couple.

5. *Case Worker* - looks into each person's background from the perspective of family, friends, community and especially ex-lovers.

Recommendations:

- One way to keep marriage fresh is to start dating your spouse again and complete the "steps to counseling" with a renewal of vows.

- Maintenance of marriages is done with post-marital counseling which should be done at least once per quarter or biannually. Marriage is not a rehabilitation centre - it cannot make imperfect perfect, you still need a neutral party to neutralize issues before they pile up.

- It is relevant for the Counselor to respect the complex nature of some relationships by consulting other specialist or just refer the client. The counselor should also be mindful that some clients may need psychotic, social, religious, medical, legal, or Crisis Intervention before proceeding with the sessions. If a negative condition is discovered do not recommend marriage. Point the person to relevant counseling. One or both may be blinded by the idea of love, help them help themselves.

- Some clients may be years-old traumatized victims of abuse and can be socially and emotionally dysfunctional. A genogram will be a helpful tool here.

- The couple should always be together in each session. The counselor's intent is to expose each client to the other, so they can make an informed decision, based on what they are learning about each other. The marriage counselor should not keep secrets for any client.

- The fact that the counseling environment belongs to the counselor, the couple should wait on the counseling outcome before finalizing engagement and marriage dates.

Pre-Marital Counseling Schedule

Session 1	Introduction	*Assignment*
	• Diagnostic Questions: Part One	
	• Bio-physical: Part One	*Yes* □
	• Open Questions and Answers	
	• Session Evaluation (Each Session	*No* □
Session 2	**Background**	*Assignment*
	• Diagnostic Questions: Part Two	
	• Bio-physical: Part Two	*Yes* □
	• Open Questions and Answers	
		No □
Session 3	**Family**	*Assignment*
	• Mother and Father	
	• Siblings	*Yes* □
	• Children	
	• Future Children	*No* □
	• Assets, Banking, Wills	
Session 4	**Communication**	*Assignment*
	• What does it mean	
	• What does it mean to me	*Yes* □
	• Allan & Jill	
	a) The Scope of Honesty	*No* □

	b) Morality c) Manipulation d) Mental Maturity	
Session 5	**Christian Marriage** • A Biblical Perspective on Marriage, Divorce & Remarriage • The Marriage Vow • Compromise versus Compensation	*Assignment* *Yes* □ *No* □
Session 6	**Civil Aspect of Marriage** • Marriage Act of the Land • Forms and Witnesses • Marriage Certificate • Simulation Exercise	*Assignment* *Yes* □ *No* □
Session 7	**Tips** • Role of the Wedding Co-ordinator • Wedding Checklist • Ceremony & Reception Places	

Diagnostic Questions

While some things take time, time takes care of some things

The interactive diagnostic questions below seek to promote critical thinking while employing an investigative style counseling. Through the reference numbers, the questions can be used randomly, sequentially or contextually. Couples can also use these questions, alternatively, to interview each other.

1. Are your parents alive?

2. Are you gainfully employed, and what is your occupation?

3. How long have you had this job?

4. How many siblings do you have and what numbered child are you?

5. Were you grown up with your parents?

6. Which of your spouse's relative is he/she closest to?

7. Why do you seek counsel?

8. Are you prepared to postpone or cancel this wedding if we discover reasonable cause?

9. Are you of the same religious persuasion?

10. Do you have children, if so, how many are living with you?

11. Have you ever received marriage counseling?

12. Do you now live in your own, rented, friend or family member's house?

13. How long have you been living at your current address?

14. What is your spouse's full name and date of birth?

15. Do you have additional means of communication (email, social media, phone number) that your spouse does not know about or cannot access?

16. Describe your childhood and teen-age days (home, school, friends, church, and pet)

17. Are you able to read and write?

18. Are you in possession of your original and certified birth certificate?

19. Is your family name your father's name?

20. Have you ever had your birth certificate adjusted by marriage, deed poll or in any form?

21. Have you altered your natural gender assignment?

22. Have you ever been married?

23. Why do you want to get married at *this* time?

24. Does your spouse rely on any family member for financial backup?

25. Have you ever been a defendant in any criminal proceedings?

26. What is your greatest fear in this relationship?

27. (Woman) Are you at this time using any form of contraceptive including tubal ligation?

28. (Man) Have you ever gotten anyone pregnant?

29. (Woman) Have you ever been pregnant?

30. (Woman) Have you ever had a miscarriage?

31. Have you ever advised anyone to terminate a pregnancy?

32. (Man) Are you fully convinced and certain that no girl has ever been impregnated by you?

33. *Are you convinced, without a shadow of doubt, that this is the person you must marry and not any other?*

34. How many relationships have you been in, within the past five years?

35. Who made the decision to break your last relationship?

36. How long ago was your last relationship?

37. Do you still communicate with any of your past lovers?

38. How does your spouse feel about any of your past lovers?

39. Do you experience regret as a result of any of your broken relationships?

40. Why do you want to marry this person?

41. Do you feel as if you are been rushed into getting married at this time?

42. How long after your last relationship did you meet your spouse?

43. Have you had any reason to rethink this relationship?

44. Is there any bad-behavior you know of and hope your spouse will change?

45. Is it okay for your spouse to keep in touch with any past lover?

46. *What do you bring into this marriage to make both your lives better socially, spiritually, psychologically, physically, academically, materially and financially?*

47. From 10, how would you rate your spouses' domestic skills?

48. Describe how your family and friends feel about this relationship?

49. Do you have any close family member or friend who has been married and is divorced, separated or is going through problems?

50. Did you offer any advice?

51. Have you ever been abused in the past of present? If yes, have you received counseling for the same?

52. Have you ever been engaged to be married?

53. Have you ever acted as counselor, to your spouse, about a relationship he/she was in?

54. Have you ever *contracted* any Sexual Transmitted Infection? If yes, have you received treatment, and do you have proof of said treatment?

55. What genre of music and movies do you like?

56. Do you like nature scene pictures?

57. Since childhood, have you ever had a same sex experience?

58. Do you prefer bright or dark colored clothing?

59. When you are home, alone, do you prefer your windows and doors closed?

60. If you have children, have you informed them of your marital intent? What were their responses?

61. Is your spouse more likely to follow advice from a close relative, a friend or from you?

62. Is there any family member or friend who believe you are not giving him/her much attention, since you met your spouse?

63. Do you think your spouse is manipulative and selfish?

64. As your spouse's parents get older and need help, are you willing to take them in your home to provide care?

65. Would it be okay for your spouse's siblings or other relatives to stay in your marital home until they *get back on their feet*?

66. Tell me about your spouse's family?

67. Tell me about your spouse's bad and good habits?

68. Is your spouse a bisexual, homosexual or heterosexual?

69. Have you ever been hospitalized? How long and for what?

70. *Is there anyone in your past you would not want to discuss during these sessions*?

71. Is there a history of any hereditary diseases or medical conditions in your spouse's family?

72. Are you a *carrier* of any Sexually Transmitted Infection?

73. Do you have any allergy or recurring illness?

74. Do you have any tattoo, spiritual or cultural marks on your body?

75. Have you, or any family member, ever been accused or convicted of a criminal offence?

76. Does anyone have any nude picture of you?

77. Are you directly or indirectly involved in contrabands of any kind?

78. Do you own or have access to a legal or illegal firearm?

79. Are you related to anyone who is involved or has been charged for any crime?

80. About how many persons do you intend to invite to your wedding ceremony?

81. Is there any experience in your past, or a family member, that still hurts you?

82. Do you have any pending court case?

83. Is your spouse a lover of children?

84. What is your current source of income?

85. Are you prepared to have joint bank accounts and assets?

86. Does your spouse appear to be a know-it-all?

87. Do you have side effects from any prescribed drugs?

88. Do you understand that mind or biological altering drug has the potential to impair your judgment, especially in time of stress or crisis and may affect you sex life?

89. Have you ever wondered if you might have been caught on a lobby or hidden camera with someone you would not want to be seen with?

90. Have you dealt with your personal *dark-closet* issues?

91. Is there anything, in your past life that you wish would never come to light?

92. Is there any experience in your past you would never want to re-experience?

93. *Is there any part of your history you would not want to talk about during these sessions?*

94. Is there anything you still do, in private, that you would not want to be discussed?

95. What are your views on pornographic materials?

96. What are your views on the use of sex toys?

97. To know more about your background, is it okay for me to ask friends or family members about you?

98. What is your spouse's work schedule?

99. Where will you live after you are married?

100. Is your current job your desired career choice?

101. Do you like your job? Do you intend changing your job?

102. Do you know of anyone who is still emotionally interested in you?

103. Do you eat meals from your spouse's parents, siblings or other relatives?

104. Do you get along with each of your family members?

105. Is there any member of your spouse's family or friends you do not like?

106. How will you fund your wedding ceremony?

107. Do you give your spouse enough time and space to be with whom he/she wills?

108. Which of you is responsible for the wedding ceremony's guest list?

109. Are you impressed by anyone's personality that you wish your spouse would have?

110. Are you satisfied with your spouse's physique?

111. Describe your spouse's character?

112. *Why do you deserve to marry this person?*

113. What is your belief about contraceptives?

114. Are you willing to give up your life of singleness to share a completely unknown future with this imperfect person?

115. *Are you prepared to live with the consequences of your choice?*

116. Is there anything you would like your spouse to clarify for you?

117. How would you feel if your spouse cannot satisfy most of your financial or sexual expectations?

118. Are you prepared to adjust property titles, assets and financial accounts to give your spouse equal authority in them?

119. Are you a beneficiary of anyone's insurance, investment or assets?

120. Are you able to calm your spouse when he/she becomes very angry?

121. Would you like to change or clarify any answer that you have given?

122. Is there anything, that we did not talk about, that you would like for us to discuss?

123. Is there any question you would like to ask your spouse?

124. Does your spouse enjoy giving to others?

125. Does your spouse hesitate to complete tasks for you but is most willing to go the extra mile for another?

126. Does your spouse display a high level of dependency on you but have another depending on him/her?

127. Is your spouse's communication usually abrupt with you but pleasant with others?

128. While in your company, does your spouse usually move away to take phone calls; use single, vague or coded words?

129. Is your spouse's smile and laughter scarce with you but is in abundance with others?

130. Does your spouse's facial expression or countenance change to frustration, anger, disgust or impatience whenever you want to talk?

131. Is your spouse uncomfortable in your company, when others are present?

132. Does your spouse keep receipts?

133. Are special dates and or events usually excused because of work or to be with other family members?

134. Does your spouse display a low level of care for you when others are present?

135. Is your spouse inquisitive about where you are and who you are with?

136. Is your spouse usually urgent to leave your company for an unknown destination?

137. Does your spouse display anxiety or unexplained, unmotivated irritable behavior when others are present?

138. Do you observe an extremely drastic turn in grooming and dress, in your spouse?

139. Is your spouse quick to blame you?

140. Is your spouse accident prone or make mistakes easily?

141. Does your spouse dislike most of your friends or want you to drop their companionship?

142. Do you feel as if your spouse takes you for granted sometimes?

143. Does your spouse appear to be an ungrateful person?

144. Does your spouse initiate or share plans for the growth of your relationship and assets?

145. Do you feel as if you are only relevant as a solution to your spouse' personal problems?

146. Does your spouse make you feel as if you are always a nuisance?

147. Does your spouse usually present you with a reason to use your resources to attend to others?

148. Does your spouse reject your suggestions or criticism but accepts that of *outsiders?*

149. Does your spouse know your fundamental spiritual belief?

150. Does your spouse appear to be willing to make sacrifices for others but not for you?

151. Is your spouse usually unapologetic?

152. Do your spouse use words such as, please, thank you, sorry or excuse me, and speak in a kind way to you?

153. Would you describe your spouse as a narcissistic person?

154. Are you in the process of buying a house or car with any relative?

155. Does your spouse easily accept his/her responsibility?

156. Do you smoke?

157. Do you drink alcoholic beverages?

158. Has any situation ever cause you to contemplate suicide?

159. Do you plan to have children?

160. How many times are you prepared to forgive your spouse if he/she cheats?

Note to the Counselor:

i.   While the counselor cannot prevent a person from getting married, or staying in a relationship, the counselor must be honest with his/her findings from the interview and share such with the couple.

ii.   The couple is not seeking counsel to determine if they are in love or not. They appear before the counselor to find out what he/she thinks about their relationship. Be more responsible about the truth than how the couple may feel about it and be certain to tell your "opinion" about their capacity to honor their vows to God.

iii.   A Marriage Counselor is a relationship referee, so when a foul is committed the appropriate flag must be raised.

iv.   The counselor should take as long as is necessary and should not be put under duress by any couple's set date.

SESSION EVALUATION

(To be completed by client)

At the end of each session the counselor should evaluate the session with the clients. Here are some recommended questions:

1. Did the counselor give you enough time to say what you wanted to say?

2. Do you think the time spent in the session was sufficient?

3. Did you get responses to the questions you asked the counselor?

4. Did the counselor appear to be rushing?

5. Did the counselor appear to be bias?

6. Do you think the questions the counselor asked you were relevant?

7. Do you think the questions the counselor asked were too intrusive?

8. Did the counselor cause you to feel comfortable, during the session?

9. Did the counselor provide you with information?

10. Did the counselor provide you with guidance?

11. Did the counselor give you relevant feedback?

12. Did the counselor provide you with hope?

13. Did the counselor provide you with support?

14. Was the environment a safe and therapeutic place to talk?

15. Did the counselor give you assignments?

16. Did the counselor give a new perspective?

17. Do you think it was worth coming to this session?

18. Would you recommend this service to others?

Assessment

1	**Appearance**	Hair	Clothing	Accessories	Healthy
		Sickly	Nails	Posture	Untidy
2	**Behaviour**	Tics	Slow	Calm	Ill-at-ease
		False	Troubled	Afraid	Energetic
		Bizarre	Tearful	Compulsive	Aggressive
3	**Attitude**	Friendly	Open	Attentive	Interested
		Evasive	Feisty	Honest	Playful
		Guarded	Defensive	Seductive	Unco-operative
		Contemptuous			
4	**Mood**	Sad	happy	Angry	Regretful
		Guilty	Depressed	Irritable	Elated
		Empty	Despairing	Anxious	Hopeless
		Pessimistic	Optimistic		
5	**Speech**	Talkative	Rapid	Slow	Pressured
		Hesitant	Dramatic	Mumbled	Staccato
		Whispered	Emotional	Difficulty	Inadequate

		Monotonous	Nonsensical	Preservation	Circumstantial
6	**Perception**	Olfactory	Visual	Auditory	Tactile
7	**Thought**				
(a)	**Process or Form of thought**	Slow	Poverty	Rapid	Flight of ideas
		Vague	Empty	Goals	Overabundance
(b)	**Content**	Erotic	Somatic	Suicidal	Preoccupation
		Obsession	Jealousy	Delusion	Compulsion
		Homicidal	Persecutory		
(c)	**Sensorial & Cognition**	Alert	Conscious		
	Orientation	Name	Time	Place	Date
	Memory	Long term	Short term	Selective	
(d)	**Literacy**	Literate	Numerate	Unlettered	
	Visio-spatial ability	Fair	Good	Excellent	Absent
	Abstract Thinking	Fair	Good	Excellent	Absent
8	**Impulse Control**				
a)	**Sexual**	Fair	Good	Excellent	Absent
b)	**Aggression**	Fair	Good	Excellent	Absent
c)	**Morality**	Fair	Good	Excellent	Absent

9 **Judgement & Insight**
- Understands likely and unlikely outcome of choices and/or actions?
- Seems pressured when making choices?
- Makes promises?

Referral Report

This is to certify that I have interviewed and counseled with

Mr._____ and

Ms._____ of

_____ and

_____ .

They were respectively born on _____

and _____ .

They have completed _____ □months □weeks □days □sessions of pre-marital counseling.

In my opinion, I believe that □they have □have not demonstrated mature characteristics and □appear □do not appear to be able to carry out marital consent.

For this reason, I am □recommending □not recommending them as mature and sober persons to be joined in holy matrimony, at this time.

_____   ____/____/____

Marriage Counselor   Date (mm/dd/yyyy)

The Marriage
Ceremony

(The Wesleyan Discipline, 1984)

Dearly beloved, we are gathered together in the sight of God, and in the presence of these witnesses, to join together this man and this woman in holy matrimony, which is an honorable estate, instituted of God. It is not be entered into unadvisedly, but reverently, discreetly, and with respect to God.

1. *Charge:* I require and charge you both, as you stand in the presence of God, to remember that love and loyalty alone will avail as the foundation of a happy and enduring home. Despite the necessary challenges that will come, your life and home can abide in joy and peace, if you faithfully keep your vows and to stay in the will of God.

2. *To: The Man* - Will you _____ have this woman to be your wedded wife, to live together after God's marital decree? Will you love, comfort, honor, and keep her, in sickness and in good health? Do you now pledge to keep yourself only to her, so long as you both shall live?

3.   ***To: The Woman*** - Will you _____ have this man to be your wedded husband, to live together after God's marital decree? Will you love, comfort, honor, and keep him, in sickness and in good health? Do you now pledge to keep yourself only to him, so long as you both shall live?

4.   ***To: The Give-A-Way Father*** - Who gives this woman to be married to the man? (This step is optional because of its Eastern patriarchal origin)

5.   ***Blessing of the Ring*** (token)

6.   **The Commitment:**

Man (while holding the woman's left hand to place the token of pledge) I, _____ take you _____, to be my wedded wife, to have and to hold, from this day forward, for better or worse, for richer or poorer, in sickness and health, to love and to cherish, and according to God's holy decree - till death do us part. (While placing the token) I therefore pledge you my faithfulness, in the name of Jesus.

Woman (while holding the man's left hand to place the token of pledge) I, _____ take you _____, to be my wedded husband, to have and to hold, from this day forward, for better or worse, for richer or poorer, in sickness and health, to love and to cherish, and according to God's holy decree - till death do us part. (While placing the token) I therefore pledge you my faithfulness, in the name of Jesus.

7. **Prayer**

8. **Signing of the Marriage Register**

9. **Declaration** –

Forasmuch as _____ and _____ have consented to vow themselves to God in holy wedlock, and pledge their faithfulness to each other, and have declared the same by exchange of tokens and the signing of civil register. I _____Marriage Officer (and any other relevant title) pronounce that _____and _____ are now husband and wife. What God has joined together, let no man put asunder.

May the Father, Son and Holy Spirit bless, preserve and keep you, Amen.

10. *Presentation of the Bridal Certificate*

Note to the officiating Minister:

11. Verify that your license is still valid (it can nullify the marriage).

12. Write the bride and groom's names from certified birth certificates.

13. Verify if, especially, the groom has his legal father's name.

14. Demand legible hand writing from bride, groom and witnesses.

15. Confirm that consent is being done by mentally competent persons who are not under duress.

16. The certificate you present at the ceremony is marked *"Bridal Copy"* because it is traditionally given to the bride by the husband as proof that he married her. Before you say *you may kiss the bride*, give the certificate to the man, then let him hand it to her (the kiss is her response).

17. Remember to officially register the marriage (within the legal time) and before the couple apply for their certified copy. Record the marriage in the church's register.

18. Be present at each wedding you are certifying with your register.

19. If during counseling you clearly identify existing and unresolved toxic issues, in the relationship, do not perform the wedding.

Sexual Intercourse

Now that you are married it is time to do the maths and be one!

"And the LORD God caused a deep sleep to fall upon Adam, and he slept, and he took one of his ribs, and closed up the flesh instead thereof. And the rib, which the LORD God had taken from man, made he a woman, and brought her unto the man. Adam said, This *is* now bone of my bones, and flesh of my flesh: she shall be called Woman, because she was taken out of man.... they shall be one flesh." (Genesis 2:21-25)

In the creative order and design, God created water which produced land; land which produced trees; trees which reproduced itself; animals which could replicate themselves. God also made a specie called Adam, mankind, "Male and female created he them; and blessed them, and called ***their name Adam***, in the day when they were created." (Genesis 5:2)

However, the male-Adam, on his own could not reproduce his specie therefore God made a female-Adam for the reproduction of their specie. The Bible describe her as an "help meet" (2:20). From this it is clear that the female was never made to be a servant to the man but partner in procreation.

A man and a woman literally become one flesh only during sexual intercourse, a time when they go back into each other. This oneness not only brings mankind into a creative mode, childbearing, but also into an expressive mode.

Sexual intercourse is the highest expression of intimacy and commitment. Embedded in this are the ingredients of a satisfying or unsatisfying relationship that can leave any human being with the widest unexplainable grin or grimace.

Between spouses,' sexual intercourse is also the highest means of emotional communication. It tells a lot about what is happing in the relationship.

Sexual intercourse is mostly beneficial when the relationship is going great. Relationship, here, includes financial, emotional, spiritual, mental, academics, physical, social and that which is mutually meaningful and significant to one or both persons.

When relationship is lacking or is causing tension it can become very pronounce during the sexual experience. It also has the power to prevent sexual intercourse.

This oneness, through sex, is the breast-milk of the union. It is many times used to measure the nutrients, vitamins, proteins and fat in the relationship. Sexual intercourse can also be the penicillin that treats a wide range of relational issues.

Sex is most gratifying when both minds are comfortable and ready to explore new dimensions your emotional worlds. For this reason, it should never be forced nor used as a reward or weapon, bribery or battle-ram or a means to merely satisfy an individual's selfish biological urges.

Sexual intercourse is also used to communicate one's emotional security. It is very common for the party who has been put on sexual redundancy to believe that the other is sharing that moment with someone else.

Incidentally, mobile devices are now caught up in love triangles as one party may believe that the other is remotely sharing sexual pleasures with others. It is one of the leading causes for the destruction of cell phones, tablets, laptops, sprain or broken fingers and wrists.

Sex is also used as a detective to find out if the other is sexually active with another person or with toys. Therefore, frequency, intensity, type, position, new behaviors and the level of sexual passion are called on to evaluate how deep one is into the other.

Those who habitually fake orgasms are really saying that they are not enjoying the experience and want the other to stop but finds it hard to say.

Sexual intercourse is truly the ultimate expression of a couples' oneness. Great sex is great communication!

Tips -

The Officiating minister is not responsible the rehearsals. Nevertheless, he should be briefed on the program, procession and recession.

Have a wedding coordinator to plan and execute the entire wedding. The coordinator should have working contact numbers for everyone involved directly and indirectly with the event. This should include owner of the venues, drivers, photographer and videographer, musicians/DJs and other mission critical personnel.

The Wedding Coordinator is the *Producer* of the event, not the couple - they are the stars!

1. Bride & Bridesmaids, Groom & Groomsmen, should dress at locations from which there is easy and alternative access to the place of the wedding and reception.

2. Travel with an emergency repair clothing kit, especially threads, hooks, buttons and a very serious glue.

3. Determine if the locations have water storage tanks and a standby power generator.

4. Determine who will assist with the dressing.

5. If any brides-maid is pregnant find out if she can manage the stress.

6. The photo shoot should not be too far from the reception area.

7. During the briefing session, inform each driver of pre-determine alternate routes.

8. Have an extra car on standby especially for the bride.

9. Transportation:

   Inbound to Place of Wedding:

   - 1 - Bride and Maid of Honor (*flower-girl)

   - 1 - Bridesmaid (*flower girl)

   - 1 - Groom and Best-Man

   - 1 - Ushers and Ring-Bearer

   - 1 - Photographer and Videographer

   Total 5 vehicles (relative to total passengers)

   Outbound to photo shoot and reception

   - 1 - Bride and Groom

   - 1 - Maid of Honor and Best Man

   - 2 - Flower girl, Bridesmaids and Groomsmen

- 1 to 2 - Parents (notify family members if they are part of the photo-shoot)

- 1 - Photographer and Videographer

Total - 6 - 7 vehicles (relative to total passengers)

The coordinator should make sure those to be in the pictures and videos are present. This will prevent time wasting, by now the bridal party may be exhausted and would love to sit.

WEDDING AND RECEPTION AREAS

If there is a usage cost be sure to sign the contract and make the necessary payments before you start dressing it. Include this in your budget.

Assign someone to dress and undress the areas.

Arrange the seating in a manner to prevent guests from walking on the bride's "red-carpet," or do not unroll it until she is ready to march in.

Inform your guests not to over-run the aisle and stage, they can spoil your photographer's shots or become a distraction.

Have ushers to protect and preserve the recessional path. Again, your photographer may want to take some exiting shots.

ROUTE AND ALTERNATE ROUTES

When necessary and if possible, acquire the necessary permit and dress the route from the place of wedding to the reception area with balloons or ribbons (non-political colors). In the invitation, inform your guests of these markers, and be sure to have someone remove them immediately after the events. If you choose to use road maps make certain they are current.

- Personal Thoughts -

"Real Things Happen to Real People in a Real World"

1. Like people, relationships age and can become unattractive.

2. You are a sum total of your good and bad habits.

3. The ability to manage relationships has been determined by your past.

4. You are in trouble if the reasons to get married changes.

5. A headache is better than a broken heart.

6. What is eating you is worse than what you eat.

7. Premarital counseling helps you to label what you are getting into, it does not prevent it.

8. If the sign says *"Dead End Ahead"* believe it. Don't waste years and resources to prove it.

9. You will never be committed if you are still searching for your ideal.

10. If mankind can cheat on God, then they can cheat on you.

11. You cannot build a relationship with someone you do not trust.

12. A lie exists because there is the truth; every lie has its truth.

13. A good relationship is all that matters in life.

14. If you appear to be an irritant to your spouse, then you are.

15. Many crave for a bear's hug - bears do not hug.

16. You may not be that significant other who makes your spouse feel happy and fulfilled.

17. Sexual intercourse is not a testimony of being satisfied.

18. The longer you take to get married the longer you stay married.

19. *Rebound* is a person who is still in love with the heartbreaker.

20. A *user* is a person waiting to cancel you.

21. *Broken-heart* is the term used for a mentally traumatized person.

22. *Cheating*: allowing or causing one person to compensate for another person perceived inefficiency; enjoying what is not yours.

23. *Depression*: a painful crave that numbs other desires.

24. *Marriage*: exciting and easy decision to make but hardest to live out.

25. *Foolish*: when you are in love with your spouse's potential.

26. *Emotional Slavery*: living your spouse's expectations.

27. *Reality*: capacity to shelf ideal.

28. *Doubt*: the downfall of any relationship.

29. *Letting go*: devoid of love or hate.

30. *Be a Man*: don't only fix the neighhor's blender.

31. *Happy*: to be in love with someone who loves more than you do.

32. *Established Communication*: background sound from your spouse's phone.

33. Learning is not doing what is expected but having a great appreciation of what must be done

34. Forgiving someone does not change his/her character. It releases you from hatred, hurt, anger, etc.

35. How your spouse solves problems is how you will be treated.

36. There are many things to do in this life and marriage is just one of them.

37. Living up to your spouse's expectation is emotional slavery.

38. Sexual intercourse is not always an expression of love.

39. Unlike medicine, relationships have unlisted side-effects.

40. Keep your head on your body when you let your hair down.

41. A person who has not been to rock-bottom has much to learn.

42. If you spend all your time fixing your weaknesses, you are weakening your strength.

43. A secret never leaves your heart.

44. Coping never dispels the issue.

45. What you don't know will always be your problem.

46. Solution fixes crisis not the damage done.

47. Things can always turn around.

48. True personalities come out in the dark.

49. You cannot be in the wrong place and expect the right things.

50. It is not good to play domino in the dark.

51. You cannot miss someone you never had.

52. Some may think you have changed when circumstances bring out the true you.

53. To go against the facts is to self-destruct.

54. Miss can change to Mrs, but mister can never change.

55. 'I do' means that you know exactly what you are getting into.

56. Samson had a plan for Delilah but did not know she had one for him; you can't blame Delilah - she was a Philistine.

57. Different games - different referees; not all Pastors are marriage counselors.

58. The attempt to make ends meet may widen the gap.

59. It is okay to lose.

60. Giving up can also be success.

61. Good health also comes from bushes not only roses. Be yourself, your worth will be discovered in time.

62. Age matters.

63. Problem-solving skills determine outcomes.

64. If you have to compete for love, it will never be yours.

65. Ego hates reality and truth.

66. Love and hate exist on the same line segment. There can be no middle grounds - you are nearer to one or the other.

67. Conversely, your spouse's past can affect your future.

68. You are most vulnerable to the one who rescues you during your emotional crisis. Marry this person and you may just be married to crosses.

69. The painful past is preserved by an inerasable memory.

70. Pride preserves problems.

71. Not all needy persons need marriages.

72. What keeps a relationship is greater than what caused it.

73. Hope is at crossroads, not at dead ends.

74. Short-temperedness and long-term goals should never be mixed.

75. Career success does not mean spousal satisfaction

Once a Man Twice a Child

The fact that marriage does not stop the aging process means that each spouse must be prepared to get older. As the body ages it will regress to resemble the frailty of a developing child. The proverbs "once a man, twice a child" encapsulates the rise and fall of the body. The following comparison is not an exhaustive list of this observable reality:

Child	Aged
Excitement for birth	Sadness at death
Born with no hair	Loss of hair
Susceptible to viruses	
Teething	Gum Issues
Born without teeth	Loss of teeth
Developing Bones	Weakening Bones

Child	Aged
Developing muscles	Loss of muscles
Developing skin	Sagging Skin
	Cannot bathe self
	Needs to be carried
	Round the clock caregiver
Demands everyone's attention	Attention seeking
	Easy to awaken
	Easily injured
	Soft/Liquid food
	Needs diapers
	Stubborn
	Know-it-all
	Possessive
No wealth	Loss of wealth
	Loves new things
	Suspicious/ Inquisitive
Cannot work	Retired

Child	Aged
Needs to be taught	
Lack of knowledge	Loss of memory
Learning to speak	Speech impairment
Crib/Bed	Bedridden

Sometimes the enthusiasm about marriage causes one to forget that one will become old, one day. Speaking about this time, the writer of Ecclesiastes had this to say, "Keep your Creator in mind while you are young! In years to come, you will be burdened down with troubles and say, "I don't enjoy life anymore" (12:1 CEV).

Conclusion -

Marriage is for those who have completed the basic necessities of life and are ready to give consent and commit a vow to God.

One should not enter Godly marriage with the idea that divorce is a backdoor out. If divorce becomes necessary one should know that such a divorce is merely a legal separation and not a death, that permits remarriage.

The need for pre-marital counseling is paramount to discover, as much as possible, a person's socialization, orientation, type of nurturing, mental and psychological health and emotional trauma, to name a few conditions.

Mankind is imperfect and not every imperfection is good for the other. Marriage, then, is a choice. The status of singleness is just as great as that of marriage. You must know which you can manage. Make that choice and be proud of it.

Marriage is one of the many things in life that you can choose to do. Do not let the invisible dictates of church, and society force you into it. Consciously own your decision for when calamity becomes the order of your day society and especially the church has no remedy.

God has given us marriage to cohabit, procreate and for recreation. It must be entered into with that consciousness that this is God's institution that must be respected. Mankind cannot look to man for human rights or the rules of marriage, it comes from God who said through Paul, "Husbands, love your wives as Christ loved the church and gave Himself up for her" (Ephesians 5:25). The marital life can only be lived according to the example of love taught and demonstrated by Jesus. Consider all that mankind has done to Him and yet He still loves them.

Face facts forget fictions, the very *'last thing'* one wants to do in life, is to get married.

About the Author

Lascelle Robinson is a Minister of Religion, Marriage Officer, Computer Technician, Author, Lecturer and a certified Search and Recovery Scuba Diver.

He holds Bachelor of Arts in Theology alongside his certificates in The Principles and Techniques in Counseling and the Laws, Policies and Procedures of the Child Protection Act of Jamaica.

He is the Dean of Students, Information Technology Specialist and Lecturer at the Caribbean Wesleyan College where he teaches Hermeneutics, Pentateuch, Introduction to the Old and New Testaments.

Among the Christian apologetics, Lascelle Robinson stands out as one who passionately debates with Bible scholars and Christian leaders with the aim of developing critical thinkers for the preservation of the Christian faith.

His favorite expression is, "Real Things Happen to Real People in a Real World."

Contact: Lascelle Robinson – facefacts02@yahoo.com

Thanks for reading! Please add a short review where you purchased this book and let me know what you thought!

www.ingramcontent.com/pod-product-compliance
Lightning Source LLC
Chambersburg PA
CBHW021202020426
42331CB00003B/173